RAG Model:

Unveiling the Mechanics of Retrieval-Augmented
Generation for Enhanced NLP Performance, Information
Retrieval, and Text Generation"

Matthew D.Passmore

Table Of Content

Introduction

The relentless pursuit of human-like interaction with machines has driven significant advancements in natural language processing (NLP). Traditional language models, despite their impressive capabilities, often falter in providing accurate, informative, and contextually relevant text. This limitation stems from their reliance solely on training data, hindering their ability to access and incorporate real-world knowledge.

Retrieval-Augmented Generation (RAG) emerges as a groundbreaking paradigm that seeks to bridge this gap. By seamlessly integrating information retrieval with natural language generation, RAG models can access and leverage external knowledge sources to produce more comprehensive and informative text. This innovative approach holds the potential to revolutionize various NLP applications, from question answering and summarization to creative writing and dialogue systems.

This paper delves into the mechanics of Retrieval-Augmented Generation, exploring its architecture, key components, and applications. We will examine the challenges and limitations associated with RAG while also highlighting promising avenues for future research. By understanding the intricacies of RAG, we aim to shed light on its potential to reshape the landscape of natural language processing.

1.1 What is Retrieval-Augmented Generation (RAG)?

Retrieval-Augmented Generation (RAG) is a powerful technique that combines the strengths of information retrieval and natural language generation. It enhances the capabilities of large language models (LLMs) by allowing them to access and incorporate external knowledge sources during the generation process.

Essentially, RAG works by:

Retrieving relevant information: When presented with a query or prompt, the RAG system first searches through a vast knowledge base to find information pertinent to the topic.

Combining information with the prompt: The retrieved information is then combined with the original query or prompt.

Generating text: The combined information is fed into a language model, which generates text based on both the original query and the newly acquired knowledge.

By augmenting the language model with external information, RAG addresses some of the limitations of traditional LLMs, such as hallucinations (generating false information) and lack of access to up-to-date data.

Key benefits of RAG include:

Improved accuracy: By grounding responses in factual information, RAG reduces the likelihood of generating incorrect or misleading content.

Enhanced relevance: RAG can provide more relevant and informative responses by accessing a broader knowledge base.

Increased flexibility: RAG can be adapted to various domains and applications by customizing the knowledge base.

1.2   Problem Statement

The advent of large language models (LLMs) has ushered in a new era of natural language processing, with these models demonstrating remarkable abilities in generating human-quality text. However, their potential is often hindered by fundamental limitations that significantly impact their real-world applicability.

Factuality and Hallucination

One of the most critical challenges facing LLMs is the propensity to generate factually incorrect or misleading information, a phenomenon commonly referred to as "hallucination." This occurs when a model generates text that is plausible but lacks grounding in real-world knowledge. Such hallucinations can have severe consequences in applications such as question answering, summarization, and information retrieval, where accuracy is paramount.

Knowledge Cutoff and Stale Information
Traditional LLMs are trained on static datasets, which means their knowledge is limited to the information available at the time of training. Consequently, they struggle to access and incorporate up-to-date information, rendering them ineffective for tasks that require current knowledge, such as news summarization or answering factual questions about recent events.

Lack of Contextual Understanding

While LLMs have shown impressive abilities in generating coherent and contextually relevant text within a given prompt, they often struggle to maintain consistency and coherence when presented with complex or ambiguous queries. This limitation arises from the challenge of effectively modeling real-world knowledge and reasoning over long text sequences.

Overreliance on Training Data

The performance of LLMs is heavily dependent on the quality and quantity of the data they are trained on. Biases present in the training data can be amplified in the generated text, leading to discriminatory or unfair outputs. Moreover, if the training data is limited in scope, the model's ability to generalize to new domains or tasks is compromised.

These limitations collectively underscore the urgent need for a more robust and reliable approach to natural language generation. A system that can access and incorporate external knowledge while maintaining factual accuracy, consistency, and adaptability is essential for addressing the shortcomings of traditional LLMs.

.

1.3   Motivation for RAG

The limitations of traditional language models have spurred the development of Retrieval-Augmented Generation (RAG) as a promising solution. The core motivation behind RAG lies in the desire to overcome the challenges posed by these models and to create more robust, informative, and reliable language generation systems.

Bridging the Gap Between Information Retrieval and

Natural Language Generation

A fundamental motivation for RAG is to unify the strengths of information retrieval and natural language generation into a cohesive framework. By combining these two disciplines, RAG aims to create systems that can effectively access and process external knowledge to enhance the quality and relevance of generated text.

Addressing the Factuality Challenge

RAG is driven by the need to mitigate the hallucination problem prevalent in traditional language models. By grounding the generation process in factual information retrieved from external sources, RAG can significantly improve the accuracy and reliability of generated text. This is particularly crucial for applications where factual correctness is paramount, such as question answering and summarization.

Enhancing Contextual Understanding

RAG seeks to improve the contextual understanding of language models by providing them with access to relevant information. By incorporating external knowledge, RAG can help models better comprehend the nuances of a given query or prompt, leading to more informative and coherent responses.

Leveraging the Power of External Knowledge
RAG recognizes the value of external knowledge sources and aims to harness their potential to augment language generation. By tapping into a vast array of information, RAG can provide models with a richer context, enabling them to generate more comprehensive and informative text.

In essence, the motivation behind RAG is to create language models that are more knowledgeable, accurate, and adaptable to various tasks and domains. By addressing the limitations of traditional models, RAG holds the promise of revolutionizing the field of natural language processing.

Retrieval-Augmented Generation (RAG) is a powerful framework that combines the strengths of information retrieval and natural language generation. To understand how RAG works, it's essential to grasp its core components and how they interact.

Overview of RAG Pipeline

A typical RAG pipeline consists of the following steps:

Input Processing: The system receives a user query or prompt as input. This input is then preprocessed to extract relevant information and potentially convert it into a suitable format for the retrieval system.

Information Retrieval: The preprocessed query is fed into a retrieval system, which searches through a vast knowledge base to find relevant information. This information can be in various formats, such as text, documents, or structured data.

Fusion: The retrieved information is combined with the original query to create a combined input for the language model. This fusion process can involve different techniques, such as concatenation, concatenation with special tokens, or more complex integration methods.

Text Generation: The combined input is fed into a language model, which generates the final text output. The model leverages both the original query and the retrieved information to produce a comprehensive and informative response.

Key Components and Their Roles

Retriever: The retriever is responsible for efficiently searching through the knowledge base and retrieving relevant information based on the input query. It employs techniques like keyword matching, semantic search, or embedding-based similarity to identify relevant documents.

Knowledge Base: The knowledge base is a repository of information that can be accessed by the retriever. It can include various types of content, such as text documents, structured data, or a combination of both.

Language Model: The language model is responsible for generating text based on the combined input from the retriever and the original query. It uses its training data and the provided information to produce coherent and informative outputs.

Interaction and Feedback Loops

RAG systems often incorporate feedback loops to improve their performance over time. For example, user feedback on generated text can be used to refine the retrieval and generation processes. Additionally, metrics such as accuracy, relevance, and coherence can be used to evaluate the system's performance and identify areas for improvement.

By understanding these core components and the overall RAG pipeline, we can gain insights into how this architecture enhances the capabilities of traditional language models.

Would you like to delve deeper into a specific component or explore RAG applications?

Sources and related content
What Is Retrieval Augmented Generation (RAG)? | Google Cloud

cloud.google.com

RAG: How Retrieval Augmented Generation Systems Work - WillowTree Apps

www.willowtreeapps.com

Enhance Your Applications with Retrieval-Augmented Generation (RAG) Architecture

hevodata.com

.

2.1 Overview of RAG Pipeline

A Retrieval-Augmented Generation (RAG) pipeline is a systematic process that combines information retrieval with natural language generation to produce informative and relevant text. It consists of several interconnected stages:

1. Input Processing

Query Formulation: The process begins with a user query or prompt, which serves as the initial input to the RAG system.

Query Preprocessing: The input query is often preprocessed to remove noise, extract keywords, or convert it into a suitable format for the subsequent retrieval stage.

2. Information Retrieval

Knowledge Base: The RAG system accesses a vast knowledge base, which can include various types of information such as text documents, structured data, or a combination of both.

Document Retrieval: Based on the preprocessed query, the retrieval system identifies and retrieves relevant documents from the knowledge base. This process typically involves techniques like keyword matching, semantic search, or embedding-based similarity.

Document Ranking: Retrieved documents are often ranked based on their relevance to the query, ensuring that the most pertinent information is presented to the language model.

3. Fusion

Contextual Enrichment: The retrieved documents are combined with the original query to create a comprehensive context for the language model.

Data Formatting: The combined information is formatted in a way that is suitable for input to the language model, such as concatenating documents with the query or creating a structured representation.

4. Text Generation

Language Model: A large language model (LLM) is employed to generate text based on the combined input. The model leverages its training data and the provided context to produce coherent and informative outputs.

Response Generation: The LLM generates text that addresses the original query while incorporating information from the retrieved documents.

5. Output Refinement (Optional)

Post-processing: In some cases, the generated text may undergo additional processing, such as summarization, fact-checking, or style adjustments, to enhance the final output.

By following these steps, a RAG pipeline effectively leverages external knowledge to improve the quality and relevance of generated text, addressing the limitations of traditional language models.

Key components of a RAG pipeline include:

Retriever: Responsible for searching and retrieving relevant information from the knowledge base.
Knowledge Base: A repository of information that can be accessed by the retriever.
Language Model: Generates text based on the combined input from the retriever and the original query.

2.2   Key Components and Their Roles

A Retrieval-Augmented Generation (RAG) system is composed of several key components that work in tandem to produce informative and relevant text.

1. Retriever
Role: The retriever is responsible for efficiently searching through the knowledge base and retrieving relevant

information based on the input query. It acts as the bridge between the user's query and the available knowledge.

Functions:

Indexes the knowledge base for efficient search.

Implements search algorithms (e.g., keyword matching, semantic search, embedding-based similarity) to find relevant documents.

Ranks retrieved documents based on their relevance to the query.

2. Knowledge Base

Role: The knowledge base serves as a repository of information that can be accessed by the retriever. It is the foundation of the RAG system, providing the factual basis for the generated text.

Types of information:

Text documents

Structured data

Multimedia content (images, videos, etc.)

Management: Effective management of the knowledge base is crucial, including updating, cleaning, and organizing information.

3. Language Model

Role: The language model is responsible for generating text based on the combined input from the retriever and the original query. It transforms the retrieved information and the user's intent into coherent and informative text.

Functions:

Processes the combined input (query and retrieved information).

Generates text based on the provided context and the language model's training data.

Ensures fluency, coherence, and relevance in the generated text.

By effectively integrating these components, a RAG system can produce high-quality outputs that are both informative and relevant to the user's query.

2.3   Interaction and Feedback Loops

A RAG system is not a static entity; it requires continuous refinement and adaptation to improve its performance. This is achieved through interaction and feedback loops that allow the system to learn and evolve.

Interaction between Components

Retriever and Language Model: The retriever and language model work in tandem to produce the final output. The retriever provides relevant information to the language model, which then generates text based on this input.

Knowledge Base and Retriever: The knowledge base is constantly updated with new information, requiring the retriever to adapt its search algorithms and indexing strategies to accommodate these changes.

User and System: The user interacts with the RAG system by providing queries or prompts. The system processes these inputs and generates responses, creating a dynamic interaction loop.

Feedback Loops

User Feedback: User feedback is invaluable for improving RAG system performance. This feedback can be explicit (e.g., ratings, comments) or implicit (e.g., clicks, time spent on the page).

System Evaluation: The system itself can evaluate its performance using various metrics, such as accuracy, relevance, and coherence. This information can be used to identify areas for improvement.

Reinforcement Learning: RAG systems can incorporate reinforcement learning techniques to optimize their performance based on rewards or penalties associated with different actions.

Benefits of Feedback Loops
Improved Accuracy: By incorporating user feedback and system evaluation, RAG systems can learn to generate more accurate and relevant responses over time.
Enhanced Relevance: Feedback loops help the system understand user preferences and tailor the generated content accordingly.

Increased Efficiency: By optimizing the retrieval and generation processes based on feedback, RAG systems can become more efficient in producing desired outputs.
Effective interaction and feedback loops are essential for creating a robust and adaptable RAG system that can continuously learn and improve its performance.

Chapter 3

Retrieval Techniques in RAG

The effectiveness of a RAG system heavily relies on the efficiency and accuracy of its retrieval component. Various techniques can be employed to extract relevant information from the knowledge base.

Traditional Retrieval Techniques

Keyword-based search: This method involves matching keywords from the query with those in the documents. While simple, it often suffers from issues like synonymy and polysemy.

Boolean search: This technique uses logical operators (AND, OR, NOT) to combine search terms and refine results. However, it can be complex for users and may not capture semantic relationships.

Dense Retrieval

Embedding-based search: This approach converts text into dense numerical vectors, representing semantic and syntactic information. By calculating the similarity between the query embedding and document embeddings, relevant documents can be retrieved.

Approximate Nearest Neighbors (ANN): To efficiently search large-scale datasets, ANN algorithms are used to find approximate nearest neighbors in the embedding space.

Hybrid Retrieval Approaches

Combination of techniques: Many systems combine traditional and dense retrieval methods to leverage their strengths. For instance, keyword-based search can be used for initial filtering, followed by dense retrieval for ranking.

Multi-stage retrieval: This approach involves multiple retrieval stages, with each stage refining the results based on different criteria or techniques.

Advanced Retrieval Techniques

Query expansion: By incorporating related terms or synonyms into the query, retrieval performance can be improved.

Re-ranking: Retrieved documents can be re-ranked based on additional factors, such as document length, freshness, or relevance feedback.

Query transformation: Using language models to reformulate the query can enhance retrieval accuracy.

Hierarchical indexing: Organizing the knowledge base into hierarchical structures can improve search efficiency.

The choice of retrieval technique depends on factors such as the size of the knowledge base, the desired level of accuracy, and computational resources. By carefully selecting and combining retrieval techniques, RAG systems can effectively extract relevant information to support the generation process.

3.1   Search Engines and Information Retrieval Systems

Information Retrieval (IR)

Information Retrieval (IR) is the field dedicated to finding and retrieving information from within large collections of data. It encompasses the science of searching for information in documents, searching for documents themselves, and searching for the metadata that describes the data.

Key concepts in IR:

Query: A formal statement of information needs, often represented as search terms.
Document: A unit of information, such as a webpage, article, or book.
Relevance: The degree to which a document satisfies the user's information need.
Ranking: The process of ordering retrieved documents based on their relevance.

Search Engines as IR Systems
Search engines are the most visible application of IR techniques. They are designed to efficiently find information on the World Wide Web.

Core components of a search engine:

Crawler: A program that explores the web, following links from page to page, and collecting information about each page encountered.

Indexer: A program that processes the collected information and creates an index, which is a structured representation of the data for efficient search.

Search engine: A software system that allows users to submit queries and returns relevant results from the index.

Challenges in IR

Vagueness: User queries are often ambiguous and can have multiple interpretations.

Relevance: Determining the true relevance of a document to a query can be subjective and challenging to measure.

Scale: The vast amount of information available on the web presents significant challenges for indexing and search.

Dynamic content: The web is constantly changing, requiring frequent updates to the search engine's index.

Beyond Web Search

While web search engines are the most prominent examples, IR techniques are applied in various domains:

Enterprise search: Finding information within an organization's internal databases.

Digital libraries: Searching for books, articles, and other scholarly materials.

E-commerce: Product search and recommendation systems.

3.2   Dense Retrieval

Dense retrieval is a modern approach to information retrieval that leverages deep learning to overcome the limitations of traditional methods like TF-IDF and BM25. Instead of relying on exact keyword matching, dense retrieval focuses on capturing the semantic and syntactic meaning of text.

How it Works

Embedding Creation: Both queries and documents are converted into dense numerical vectors, often referred to as embeddings. These embeddings represent the semantic and syntactic meaning of the text.

Similarity Calculation: The similarity between the query embedding and document embeddings is calculated. This is typically done using cosine similarity, which measures the cosine of the angle between two vectors.

Retrieval: Documents with the highest similarity scores to the query are retrieved as relevant results.
Advantages of Dense Retrieval

Semantic Understanding: Dense retrieval can capture semantic relationships between words, allowing it to retrieve documents that are semantically similar to the query, even if they don't share exact keywords.

Improved Relevance: By considering the overall meaning of the text, dense retrieval often produces more relevant results compared to traditional methods.

Handling Long-Tail Queries: Dense retrieval is particularly effective for handling complex and ambiguous queries, known as long-tail queries.

Challenges and Considerations

Computational Cost: Creating and storing embeddings for large datasets can be computationally expensive.

Evaluation: Evaluating the performance of dense retrieval systems can be challenging due to the lack of standard benchmarks.

Data Quality: The quality of the embeddings is highly dependent on the quality of the training data.

Popular Techniques

Dense Passage Retrieval (DPR): A framework for open-domain question answering that uses dense retrieval to find relevant passages.

Sentence-BERT: A pre-trained model for generating sentence embeddings.

Approximate Nearest Neighbor Search (ANN): Efficiently finding similar items in large datasets.

Dense retrieval has shown promising results in various applications, including information retrieval, question answering, and recommendation systems. As the field continues to evolve, we can expect to see even more advanced and effective dense retrieval techniques emerge.

3.3   Hybrid Retrieval Approaches

Hybrid retrieval combines the strengths of traditional and dense retrieval methods to enhance overall search performance. By leveraging the complementary advantages of both approaches, hybrid systems can often deliver more accurate and comprehensive results.

Combining Traditional and Dense Retrieval
Sequential Combination: In this approach, traditional retrieval is used to filter the document corpus initially, followed by dense retrieval to rank the remaining documents.

Parallel Combination: Both traditional and dense retrieval methods are applied independently, and their results are merged using techniques like rank fusion or document re-ranking.

Hybrid Model: A single model combines traditional and dense retrieval components within a unified framework, allowing for more complex interactions and optimizations.

Fusion Techniques

Rank Fusion: Assigns weights to the ranking scores from different retrieval methods and combines them into a single score.

Document Re-ranking: Reorders the combined list of documents based on additional factors or relevance criteria.
Cascade Model: Combines multiple retrieval stages, with each stage refining the results based on specific criteria.
..
Challenges and Considerations
Complexity: Hybrid retrieval systems can be more complex to design and implement compared to single-method approaches.

Parameter Tuning: Balancing the contributions of different retrieval methods requires careful parameter tuning.
Evaluation: Measuring the effectiveness of hybrid retrieval can be challenging due to the combination of different metrics.

Benefits of Hybrid Retrieval

Improved Accuracy: By combining the strengths of both traditional and dense retrieval, hybrid systems can achieve higher accuracy and recall.

Enhanced Robustness: Hybrid approaches can be more robust to different types of queries and data distributions.

Flexibility: Hybrid systems can be adapted to various search scenarios and domains.

Example Use Cases

Enterprise search: Combining keyword-based search with semantic understanding for efficient information retrieval within an organization.

E-commerce: Using hybrid retrieval to improve product search and recommendation systems.

Academic search: Combining traditional bibliographic search with semantic-based document retrieval for scholarly research.

By carefully considering the specific requirements of a search application, hybrid retrieval can provide significant performance improvements over traditional or dense retrieval methods alone.

?

Chapter 4
Knowledge Base Construction and Management

A robust knowledge base is the cornerstone of an effective RAG system. It serves as the repository of information that the retriever accesses to find relevant content. Building and maintaining a high-quality knowledge base is crucial for the overall performance of the system.

Knowledge Acquisition and Curation
Data Sources: Identify and access diverse data sources, including text documents, structured data, and potentially multimedia content.

Data Extraction: Extract relevant information from various formats (e.g., PDFs, HTML, databases) using appropriate tools and techniques.

Data Cleaning: Remove noise, inconsistencies, and errors from the extracted data to ensure data quality.
Data Enrichment: Enhance data with additional information, such as metadata, annotations, or external knowledge sources.

Knowledge Base Organization and Indexing

Structure: Define the structure of the knowledge base based on the specific application and user needs. Consider using hierarchical, graph-based, or hybrid structures.

Indexing: Create efficient indexes to facilitate fast retrieval of relevant information. Popular indexing techniques include inverted indexes, term frequency-inverse document frequency (TF-IDF), and embeddings.

.

Metadata: Assign appropriate metadata to documents to enable efficient search and filtering.

Knowledge Base Updates and Maintenance

Data Ingestion: Develop a process for continuously ingesting new information into the knowledge base.

Data Validation: Implement mechanisms to ensure the quality and consistency of newly added data.

Data Expiration: Define policies for removing outdated or irrelevant information from the knowledge base.

Knowledge Graph Construction: Consider building a knowledge graph to represent relationships between entities and concepts.

Challenges in Knowledge Base Management

Data Quality: Maintaining high-quality data is essential but challenging due to noise, inconsistencies, and biases.

Scalability: Handling large-scale knowledge bases requires efficient storage and retrieval techniques.

Knowledge Acquisition: Extracting information from various sources can be time-consuming and labor-intensive.

.

Knowledge Representation: Choosing the appropriate representation for knowledge can impact retrieval effectiveness.

By effectively addressing these challenges and following best practices, organizations can build and maintain high-quality knowledge bases that support the success of their RAG systems.

4.1 Knowledge Acquisition and Curation

The foundation of a robust RAG system lies in the quality and quantity of its knowledge base. Knowledge acquisition and curation are critical processes in building a valuable information repository.

Knowledge Acquisition

Knowledge acquisition is the process of gathering information from various sources to populate the knowledge base. Effective knowledge acquisition involves:

Identifying Relevant Sources: Determining the most suitable data sources based on the specific domain and requirements of the RAG system. This can include:

Textual data: Books, articles, reports, websites, social media
Structured data: Databases, spreadsheets, APIs

Unstructured data: Images, videos, audio

Data Extraction: Employing techniques to extract relevant information from different data formats. This may involve: Web scraping: Extracting data from websites

Text mining: Analyzing textual data to extract keywords, entities, and relationships
Data parsing: Converting data from one format to another
API integration: Accessing data through application programming interfaces
Data Integration: Combining data from multiple sources into a unified format for storage in the knowledge base.

Knowledge Curation
Once data is acquired, it undergoes a curation process to ensure quality and relevance:

Data Cleaning: Removing noise, inconsistencies, and errors from the data to improve its accuracy and reliability.

Data Enrichment: Adding context, metadata, or additional information to enhance the value of the data.

Data Standardization: Converting data into a consistent format for efficient processing and analysis.

Data Validation: Verifying the accuracy and completeness of the data to maintain data quality.

Data Quality Assessment: Evaluating the overall quality of the knowledge base and identifying areas for improvement.

Challenges and Considerations
Data Volume: Dealing with large volumes of data can be computationally intensive and requires efficient storage and processing techniques.

Data Quality: Ensuring data accuracy, consistency, and completeness is crucial for the reliability of the RAG system.

Data Bias: Addressing biases in the data is essential to prevent the system from generating biased outputs.
Data Privacy: Protecting sensitive information and complying with privacy regulations is crucial.
Data Lifecycle Management: Effective management of data throughout its lifecycle, including creation, storage, retrieval, and disposal, is essential.

By effectively addressing these challenges, organizations can build high-quality knowledge bases that support the development of robust and reliable RAG systems.

4.2   Knowledge Base Organization and Indexing

Effective organization and indexing of the knowledge base are crucial for efficient retrieval and utilization of information. A well-structured knowledge base enhances search performance and user experience.

Knowledge Base Organization
Hierarchical Structure: Organizing information into a hierarchical structure, similar to a file system, can improve navigation and search. This structure can be based on topics, categories, or subject areas.

Ontology-Based Structure: Using ontologies to represent knowledge can provide a more semantic and structured approach. Ontologies define classes, properties, and relationships between concepts, enabling more precise queries and inferences.

Graph-Based Structure: Representing knowledge as a graph, where nodes represent entities and edges represent relationships, can capture complex connections between information. This structure is particularly useful for knowledge graphs.

Indexing

.

Inverted Index: This is a common indexing technique that maps words to the documents containing them. It allows for efficient retrieval of documents based on keyword searches.

Embedding-Based Indexing: Converting documents into dense vector representations (embeddings) enables semantic search, where similar documents are retrieved based on their meaning.

Hybrid Indexing: Combining inverted indexes and embeddings can offer the best of both worlds, providing efficient keyword-based search and semantic understanding. Faceting: Creating additional indexes based on specific attributes (e.g., author, date, topic) can facilitate filtering and refining search results.

Challenges and Considerations

Scalability: As the knowledge base grows, efficient indexing and retrieval become increasingly challenging.

Dynamic Content: Handling updates and changes to the knowledge base requires efficient indexing and re-indexing mechanisms.

Query Complexity: Supporting complex queries, such as natural language queries or faceted search, requires advanced indexing techniques.

By carefully considering the specific requirements of the RAG system, organizations can choose the most appropriate organization and indexing strategies to optimize knowledge retrieval.

4.3   Knowledge Base Updates and Maintenance

A dynamic knowledge base is essential for a RAG system to remain relevant and effective. Continuous updates and maintenance are crucial to ensure data freshness, accuracy, and completeness.

Data Ingestion
..
Data Sources Monitoring: Regularly check for updates in existing data sources.

New Data Identification: Identify new relevant data sources to expand the knowledge base.

Data Extraction: Employ efficient methods to extract new information from identified sources.

Data Transformation: Convert new data into a compatible format for integration into the knowledge base.

Data Validation and Quality Control
Data Cleaning: Remove inconsistencies, errors, and duplicates from newly acquired data.

Data Enrichment: Add missing information or context to enhance data value.
Data Verification: Validate the accuracy and reliability of the updated data.

Quality Metrics: Establish metrics to measure data quality and track improvements.

Knowledge Base Updates

Incremental Updates: Incorporate new information into the existing knowledge base without disrupting the overall structure.

Index Updates: Update indexes to reflect changes in the knowledge base.

Metadata Updates: Modify metadata to reflect changes in document content or attributes.

Schema Evolution: Adapt the knowledge base schema to accommodate new data types or structures.

Data Expiration and Archiving

Data Retention Policies: Define policies for retaining and archiving data based on its value and age.

Data Expiration: Remove outdated or irrelevant information to optimize storage and retrieval.

Data Archiving: Store historical data for potential future use or compliance purposes.

Challenges and Considerations

Data Volume: Managing large volumes of incoming data can be computationally intensive.

Data Quality: Maintaining high data quality over time requires ongoing effort and validation.

Change Management: Effectively managing changes to the knowledge base without disrupting the system is crucial.

Resource Allocation: Allocating sufficient resources for knowledge base updates and maintenance is essential.

By implementing effective knowledge base update and maintenance practices, organizations can ensure that their RAG systems have access to the most current and relevant information, leading to improved performance and user satisfaction.

Chapter 5
Generator Models for RAG

The generator model is a critical component of a RAG system, responsible for transforming the retrieved information and the original query into coherent and informative text. Various types of language models can be employed as generators.

Pre-trained Language Models (PLMs)
Transformer Architecture: Most modern language models are based on the transformer architecture, which excels at capturing long-range dependencies in text.
Transfer Learning: PLMs are typically pre-trained on massive amounts of text data, allowing them to acquire a general language understanding. This pre-training enables efficient fine-tuning for specific tasks.
Examples: GPT-3, BERT, Jurassic-1 Jumbo
Sequence-to-Sequence Models
Encoder-Decoder Structure: These models consist of an encoder that processes the input sequence (combined query and retrieved documents) and a decoder that generates the output sequence.

Attention Mechanism: Attention allows the decoder to focus on relevant parts of the input sequence, improving the quality of generated text.

Examples: Transformer models like BART, T5
Generative Adversarial Networks (GANs)
Generator and Discriminator: GANs employ a generative model to create text and a discriminative model to evaluate its quality. Through adversarial training, the generator learns to produce more realistic and diverse text.

Applications in RAG: GANs can be used to generate different text variations based on the same input, enhancing creativity and diversity.

Key Considerations for Generator Models

Model Capacity: The size and complexity of the language model influence its ability to handle complex queries and generate detailed responses.
Fine-tuning: Adapting the model to specific domains or tasks through fine-tuning is crucial for optimal performance.
Evaluation Metrics: Selecting appropriate metrics to assess the quality of generated text is essential for model improvement.

Computational Resources: Training and deploying large language models require substantial computational resources.

By carefully selecting and fine-tuning the generator model, RAG systems can achieve high-quality outputs that meet the specific requirements of different applications.

5.1   Pre-trained Language Models (PLMs)

Pre-trained Language Models (PLMs) have revolutionized the field of Natural Language Processing (NLP). These models are trained on massive amounts of text data to learn general language representations. This pre-training process enables them to be adapted to various downstream tasks with minimal fine-tuning.

How PLMs Work

Self-supervised learning: PLMs are typically trained using self-supervised learning techniques, where the model learns to predict masked words or reconstruct corrupted text. This process allows the model to capture rich linguistic patterns and representations.

Transformer architecture: Most state-of-the-art PLMs are based on the transformer architecture, which is particularly effective at capturing long-range dependencies in text.

Pre-training on massive datasets: PLMs are trained on vast amounts of text data, allowing them to learn general language understanding and world knowledge.

Benefits of PLMs

Improved performance: PLMs often outperform traditional NLP models on a wide range of tasks, including text classification, question answering, and machine translation.

Faster development: Fine-tuning a pre-trained model is generally faster and requires less data compared to training a model from scratch.

Transfer learning: PLMs can be adapted to new tasks and domains with minimal additional training.

Popular PLMs

BERT: Bidirectional Encoder Representations from Transformers, capable of capturing contextual information from both directions.

GPT: Generative Pre-trained Transformer, designed for text generation tasks.

RoBERTa: Robustly Optimized BERT Pretraining Approach, an improved version of BERT with enhanced training procedures.

T5: Text-to-Text Transfer Transformer, a versatile model that can be adapted to various NLP tasks.

Applications of PLMs in RAG

Text generation: PLMs can generate informative and coherent text based on the retrieved information and the original query.

Query understanding: PLMs can help to better understand the user's intent and extract relevant information from the query.

Contextualization: PLMs can incorporate contextual information from the retrieved documents into the generated text.

Summarization: PLMs can be used to summarize retrieved documents or generate concise answers to queries.

By leveraging the power of PLMs, RAG systems can achieve significant improvements in terms of accuracy, coherence, and relevance of generated text.

5.2 Sequence-to-Sequence Models

Sequence-to-sequence (Seq2Seq) models are a class of neural network architectures designed to transform one sequence of data into another sequence. They are particularly useful for tasks where the input and output lengths are variable, such as machine translation, text summarization, and question answering.

Architecture

A Seq2Seq model typically consists of two main components:

Encoder: This part of the model processes the input sequence and converts it into a fixed-length vector representation, often called a context vector. Recurrent Neural Networks (RNNs), especially Long Short-Term Memory (LSTM) and Gated Recurrent Units (GRU), were commonly used in earlier models, but attention mechanisms have become the preferred choice.

Decoder: The decoder generates the output sequence one element at a time, conditioned on the context vector and previously generated output tokens. It can also employ attention mechanisms to focus on different parts of the input sequence during decoding.

Attention Mechanism
Attention has been a game-changer for Seq2Seq models. It allows the decoder to focus on specific parts of the input sequence while generating each output token. This mechanism helps capture long-range dependencies and improves the quality of the generated output.

Applications of Seq2Seq Models in RAG

Text Generation: Seq2Seq models can be used to generate human-quality text based on the combined input of the query and retrieved documents.

Summarization: Generating concise summaries of retrieved documents is a natural fit for Seq2Seq models.

Question Answering: By treating the question as input and the retrieved documents as context, Seq2Seq models can generate informative and relevant answers.

Challenges and Considerations
Vanishing Gradient Problem: RNNs can suffer from the vanishing gradient problem, making it difficult to learn long-term dependencies. Attention mechanisms help mitigate this issue.

Exposure Bias: During training, the decoder is fed with ground truth tokens, which can lead to exposure bias during inference. Beam search is often used to address this.

Model Complexity: Seq2Seq models can be computationally expensive to train and deploy.

While PLMs have gained significant popularity, Seq2Seq models still have their place in specific applications, especially when fine-grained control over the generation process is required.

5.3   Generative Adversarial Networks (GANs)

Generative Adversarial Networks (GANs) are a class of machine learning frameworks that pit two neural networks against each other in a competitive process. This adversarial setup leads to the generation of remarkably realistic data.

How GANs Work
A GAN consists of two main components:

Generator: This neural network generates new data instances. It starts with random noise as input and aims to produce data that resembles the training data.
Discriminator: This network acts as a classifier, determining whether the input data is real (from the training set) or fake (generated by the generator).

The generator and discriminator are trained simultaneously in a competitive process. The generator's goal is to produce data that can fool the discriminator, while the discriminator aims to accurately classify real and fake data. This adversarial process drives both networks to improve over time, resulting in the generator producing increasingly realistic data.

Applications of GANs
Image Generation: GANs have excelled in generating highly realistic images, including faces, landscapes, and objects.
Video Generation: Creating realistic videos is a challenging task, but GANs have shown promising results in generating short video clips.

Data Augmentation: GANs can be used to generate synthetic data to augment training datasets, improving model performance.

Style Transfer: Transforming the style of one image to match the style of another image.

Text-to-Image Generation: Generating images based on textual descriptions.

Challenges with GANs

Training Instability: GANs can be challenging to train, often suffering from mode collapse or vanishing gradients.

Evaluation: Assessing the quality of generated data can be subjective and difficult to quantify.

Mode Collapse: The generator might collapse to produce only a limited set of samples, reducing diversity.

Despite these challenges, GANs have shown remarkable potential and continue to be an active area of research.

GANs in RAG

While GANs have not been widely adopted in RAG systems as of now, they offer potential benefits:

Data Augmentation: Generating synthetic training data can improve the performance of the retriever and language model.

Text Variation: GANs could be used to generate different text variations based on the same input, increasing diversity in the output.

Improved Generation Quality: By training a GAN on a large dataset of generated text, the quality of the output from the RAG system could potentially be enhanced.

However, the challenges associated with GAN training and evaluation need to be carefully considered before applying them in a RAG context.

Chapter 6
RAG Applications and Use Cases

Retrieval-Augmented Generation (RAG) offers a versatile framework with applications across various domains. By combining the strengths of information retrieval and natural language generation, RAG systems can address complex challenges and deliver improved performance.

Question Answering

Open-Domain Question Answering: RAG can access a vast knowledge base to provide comprehensive and informative answers to a wide range of questions.

Factual Question Answering: By grounding answers in factual information, RAG can enhance the accuracy and reliability of question answering systems.

Domain-Specific Question Answering: RAG can be tailored to specific domains (e.g., medicine, law) to provide expert-level answers.

Summarization

Document Summarization: RAG can generate concise and informative summaries of lengthy documents by extracting key information.

News Summarization: Creating summaries of news articles can be effectively achieved using RAG, providing users with quick overviews.

Meeting Summarization: Generating summaries of meetings can improve productivity and knowledge sharing.

Text Generation

Creative Writing: RAG can assist in creative writing tasks by providing relevant information and inspiration.

Storytelling: By combining factual knowledge with storytelling techniques, RAG can generate engaging narratives.

Dialogue Systems: RAG-powered chatbots can access external knowledge to provide more informative and engaging conversations.

Other Applications

Customer Service: RAG can enhance customer service chatbots by providing access to product information, troubleshooting guides, and customer support history.

Search Engines: RAG can improve search results by providing relevant summaries and information snippets.
Education: RAG can be used to create personalized learning experiences by adapting content to individual student needs.

Market Research: RAG can analyze market data and generate insights to support decision-making.

Challenges and Considerations

Knowledge Base Quality: The quality of the knowledge base significantly impacts the performance of the RAG system.
Hallucinations: Preventing the generation of false or misleading information remains a challenge.

Computational Resources: Training and deploying large-scale RAG systems require substantial computational power.

Ethical Considerations: Ensuring fairness, bias mitigation, and privacy protection is crucial.

By addressing these challenges and leveraging the potential of RAG, organizations can unlock new opportunities and improve the efficiency of various applications.

6.1   Question Answering

.

Question Answering (QA) is a subfield of natural language processing (NLP) and information retrieval (IR) that focuses on building systems capable of automatically answering questions posed by humans in natural language.

Types of Question Answering

Closed-domain QA: Systems designed to answer questions within a specific domain or knowledge base. Examples include medical QA systems, legal QA systems, or customer support chatbots.

Open-domain QA: Systems that aim to answer questions from any domain, relying on vast amounts of unstructured text data. These systems require advanced natural language understanding and information retrieval capabilities.

Challenges in Question Answering

Question Understanding: Accurately interpreting the user's intent and question type is crucial.

Answer Extraction: Identifying the correct answer within a document or knowledge base can be complex, especially for factual questions.

Contextual Understanding: Understanding the context of a question is essential for providing relevant and accurate answers.

Evaluation: Measuring the quality of answers can be subjective and challenging.

RAG and Question Answering

Retrieval-Augmented Generation (RAG) has significantly impacted the field of question answering by providing a powerful framework for accessing and utilizing external knowledge sources. By combining information retrieval with language generation, RAG systems can:

Improve accuracy: By grounding answers in factual information, RAG can reduce the likelihood of hallucinations.

Enhance comprehensiveness: RAG can provide more comprehensive and informative answers by leveraging external knowledge.

Address different question types: RAG can handle a wider range of question types, including factual, definitional, and how-to questions.

Evaluation Metrics
Common evaluation metrics for question answering systems include:

Exact Match (EM): Measures the percentage of answers that exactly match the ground truth answer.
F1-score: Combines precision and recall to evaluate the overall performance.
BLEU: Used for evaluating the quality of generated answers, especially for open-ended questions.

By addressing the challenges and leveraging the potential of RAG, question answering systems can continue to improve and provide increasingly valuable support to users.

6.2 Summarization

Summarization is the process of condensing a text into a shorter version while preserving its essential information. It involves identifying the main points and discarding redundant or less important details.

Types of Summarization

Extractive Summarization: This approach selects sentences or phrases directly from the original text to form the summary.

Abstractive Summarization: This involves generating new text that captures the meaning of the original text, often requiring deeper language understanding.

Query-based Summarization: Focuses on generating summaries relevant to a specific query or topic.

Challenges in Summarization

Information Loss: Deciding which information to include and exclude can be challenging.
Preserving Coherence: Maintaining the overall structure and coherence of the original text in the summary is crucial.

Handling Different Text Formats: Summarizing various text formats (news articles, research papers, social media posts) requires different approaches.

RAG and Summarization
RAG systems can significantly enhance summarization capabilities by:

Providing Contextual Understanding: By accessing relevant information from a knowledge base, RAG can generate more informative and accurate summaries.

Handling Long Documents: RAG can effectively summarize lengthy documents by breaking them down into smaller segments and combining the summaries.

Adapting to Different Summarization Tasks: RAG can be customized to generate different types of summaries based on user needs.

Evaluation Metrics

Common evaluation metrics for summarization include:

ROUGE: Evaluates the overlap between the generated summary and reference summaries.

BLEU: Originally designed for machine translation, but also used for summarization evaluation.

METEOR: Combines exact and stemmed word matching with synonymy and paraphrase detection.

By addressing the challenges and leveraging the potential of RAG, summarization systems can provide valuable tools for information processing and dissemination.

6.3   Text Generation

Text generation is the process of automatically producing human-like text, ranging from simple sentences to complex documents. It's a subfield of natural language processing (NLP) that has seen significant advancements with the development of deep learning models.

Types of Text Generation

Creative Text Generation: This involves generating original and imaginative text, such as poetry, storytelling, or scriptwriting.

Informative Text Generation: This focuses on generating factual and informative text, like summaries, reports, or product descriptions.

Conversational Text Generation: This involves creating human-like dialogue for chatbots or virtual assistants.

Code Generation: Generating code snippets or entire programs based on natural language descriptions.

Challenges in Text Generation

Coherence: Maintaining consistency and logical flow throughout the generated text.

Factuality: Ensuring that generated text is accurate and aligned with real-world knowledge.

Diversity: Producing a variety of text formats and styles.

Evaluation: Developing effective metrics to assess the quality of generated text.

RAG and Text Generation

RAG systems can enhance text generation by:

Providing Factual Grounding: By incorporating information from a knowledge base, RAG can improve the accuracy and relevance of generated text.

Enhancing Creativity: Access to a vast amount of information can inspire new ideas and creative approaches to text generation.

Supporting Different Text Formats: RAG can be adapted to generate various text formats by combining information from different sources.

Applications of Text Generation

Content Creation: Generating articles, blog posts, social media content, and marketing copy.

Language Translation: Translating text from one language to another.

Chatbots and Virtual Assistants: Creating engaging and informative conversations.
Education: Generating personalized learning materials and tutoring systems.
Creative Writing: Assisting writers in generating ideas, plotlines, or characters.

Text generation is a rapidly evolving field with immense potential. As models become more sophisticated, we can expect to see even more impressive and creative applications emerge.

6.4   Other Applications

Beyond the core applications we've discussed (question answering, summarization, text generation), RAG has a wide range of potential applications across various industries.

Information Retrieval

Enhanced Search: RAG can improve search results by providing summaries, relevant snippets, or even generating answers directly from retrieved documents.

Personalized Search: By understanding user preferences and context, RAG can deliver more tailored search results.

Customer Service

Chatbots: RAG-powered chatbots can access a knowledge base to provide accurate and informative responses to customer inquiries.

Product Recommendations: By analyzing customer behavior and preferences, RAG can suggest relevant products or services.

Education

Personalized Learning: RAG can create customized learning materials based on student needs and preferences.

Intelligent Tutoring Systems: RAG-powered tutors can provide explanations, examples, and feedback to students.

Market Research

Sentiment Analysis: RAG can analyze customer feedback and social media data to extract insights and trends.

Competitive Analysis: By comparing products or services, RAG can help identify market opportunities.

Healthcare

Medical Question Answering: RAG can provide information about diseases, symptoms, and treatments.

Drug Discovery: By analyzing medical literature, RAG can assist in identifying potential drug targets.

Legal

Legal Research: RAG can help lawyers find relevant case law and legal precedents.

Document Summarization: RAG can summarize legal documents, making it easier for lawyers to understand complex cases.

Financial Services

Risk Assessment: RAG can analyze financial data to identify potential risks.

Investment Research: RAG can gather and analyze financial information to support investment decisions.

These are just a few examples of the many potential applications of RAG. As the technology continues to evolve, we can expect to see even more innovative and impactful uses emerge.

Chapter 7
Evaluation Metrics for RAG Systems

Evaluating the performance of a RAG system requires a comprehensive approach that considers both the retrieval and generation components. Here are key metrics to assess different aspects of a RAG system:

Retrieval Evaluation

Precision: The proportion of retrieved documents that are relevant to the query.

Recall: The proportion of relevant documents that are successfully retrieved.

F1-score: A harmonic mean of precision and recall.

Mean Average Precision (MAP): Measures the average precision at different recall levels.

Normalized Discounted Cumulative Gain (NDCG): Considers the position of relevant documents in the ranked list.

Generation Evaluation

BLEU (Bilingual Evaluation Understudy): Measures the overlap between the generated text and reference summaries.

ROUGE: Similar to BLEU, but focuses on n-gram matches.
METEOR: Combines exact and stemmed word matching with synonymy and paraphrase detection.

Human Evaluation: Subjective assessment of the quality of generated text by human experts.

Factuality and Coherence

Fact-checking: Verifying the accuracy of information presented in the generated text.

Consistency: Evaluating the logical consistency of the generated text.
Hallucination Detection: Identifying instances where the system generates false or misleading information.

Additional Metrics
Response Time: Measuring the time taken to generate a response.

Cost-Effectiveness: Assessing the computational cost of the RAG system.

User Satisfaction: Gathering feedback from users to measure the overall system performance.

Challenges in Evaluation

Subjectivity: Human evaluation can be subjective and inconsistent.

Dynamic Nature of Language: Language is constantly evolving, making it challenging to develop static evaluation metrics.

Multiple Dimensions: Evaluating RAG systems requires considering various aspects, such as factual accuracy, coherence, and relevance.

By combining these metrics and considering the specific goals of the RAG system, it is possible to obtain a comprehensive evaluation of its performance. It's important to note that no single metric can capture all aspects of RAG system quality, and a combination of metrics is often necessary.

7.1 Retrieval Effectiveness

Retrieval effectiveness measures how well a system can find relevant information in response to a query. It is a crucial aspect of information retrieval and significantly impacts the overall performance of a RAG system.

Key Metrics

Precision: The proportion of retrieved documents that are actually relevant to the query.

Formula: Precision = (Number of relevant documents retrieved) / (Total number of documents retrieved)

Recall: The proportion of relevant documents in the entire collection that were actually retrieved.

Formula: Recall = (Number of relevant documents retrieved) / (Total number of relevant documents)

F1-score: A harmonic mean of precision and recall, providing a balanced measure.

Formula: F1-score = 2 * (Precision * Recall) / (Precision + Recall)

Beyond Precision and Recall

While precision and recall are fundamental, other metrics offer additional insights:

Mean Average Precision (MAP): Considers the order of retrieved documents, assigning higher weights to documents ranked higher.
Normalized Discounted Cumulative Gain (NDCG): Similar to MAP, but also considers the relevance level of documents.

R-precision: Measures the precision at the rank equal to the total number of relevant documents.

Challenges in Evaluating Retrieval Effectiveness

Relevance Judgment: Determining whether a document is truly relevant to a query can be subjective and time-consuming.

Query Diversity: Different users may have different interpretations of the same query, affecting relevance judgments.

Dynamic Content: Changes in the document collection over time can impact retrieval effectiveness.

Improving Retrieval Effectiveness
Relevance Feedback: Incorporating user feedback to refine search results.
Query Expansion: Expanding the original query with related terms to improve recall.
Document Representation: Using effective document representations (e.g., embeddings) to enhance similarity calculations.

Evaluation Methodology: Employing appropriate evaluation metrics and experimental designs.

By carefully considering these factors and utilizing appropriate metrics, organizations can effectively measure and improve the retrieval performance of their RAG systems.

7.2   Generation Quality

Generation quality refers to the overall quality of the text produced by a language model. It encompasses various aspects, including fluency, coherence, relevance, and factuality.

Key Metrics

BLEU (Bilingual Evaluation Understudy): Originally designed for machine translation, BLEU is widely used to evaluate the quality of generated text. It measures the overlap between n-grams in the generated text and reference text.

ROUGE (Recall-Oriented Understudy for Gisting Evaluation): Specifically designed for summarization,

ROUGE also evaluates the overlap of n-grams between the generated and reference text.

METEOR (Metric for Evaluation of Translation with Explicit Ordering): Combines exact and stemmed word matching with synonymy and paraphrase detection.

CIDEr (Consensus-based Image Description Evaluation): Initially developed for image captioning, CIDEr has been adapted for text generation evaluation.

Other Considerations

Beyond these metrics, other factors contribute to generation quality:

Fluency: The text should be grammatically correct and read smoothly.
Coherence: The text should be logically connected and make sense in context.

Relevance: The generated text should be relevant to the given prompt or topic.

Factuality: For informative text, accuracy is crucial.

Creativity: For creative text generation, originality and diversity are important.

Challenges in Evaluating Generation Quality

Subjectivity: Human judgment is often required to assess certain aspects of text quality, such as creativity or coherence.

Reference Bias: Reliance on reference text can limit the evaluation of truly novel or creative outputs.

Multiple Dimensions: Text quality encompasses various aspects, making it challenging to capture with a single metric.

Improving Generation Quality

Model Architecture: Choosing the right model architecture and hyperparameters is crucial.
Data Quality: High-quality training data is essential for producing high-quality text.
Fine-tuning: Adapting the model to specific tasks and domains can improve performance.
Human-in-the-loop: Incorporating human feedback can help refine the model.

By carefully considering these factors and employing a combination of metrics, researchers and developers can effectively evaluate and improve the quality of generated text.

.

7.3   Factuality and Coherence

Factuality and coherence are two critical dimensions of text quality, particularly important in the context of RAG systems.

Factuality
Factuality refers to the accuracy of the information presented in the generated text. It is essential for building trust and credibility.

Challenges:

Hallucinations: Language models can generate plausible-sounding but incorrect information.

Data Bias: Bias in the training data can lead to biased and inaccurate outputs.

Knowledge Base Quality: The accuracy of the information in the knowledge base directly impacts the factuality of the generated text.

Strategies for Improvement:

Fact-checking: Implementing mechanisms to verify information against reliable sources.
Citation: Providing references for claims to enhance credibility.
Confidence Estimation: Estimating the model's confidence in the generated text to identify potential inaccuracies.

Coherence
Coherence refers to the logical flow and consistency of the generated text. It ensures that the text is easy to understand and follow.

Challenges:

Logical Reasoning: Maintaining logical consistency across different parts of the text.
Reference Resolution: Correctly referring to entities and concepts throughout the text.

Discourse Structure: Organizing information in a clear and structured manner.

Strategies for Improvement:

Contextual Understanding: Utilizing models that can effectively capture and process contextual information.
Discourse Markers: Employing language markers to indicate relationships between sentences.
Evaluation Metrics: Developing metrics that specifically assess coherence.

The Role of RAG in Factuality and Coherence

RAG systems can contribute to improving both factuality and coherence by:

Grounding in Knowledge: Accessing external knowledge sources can help ensure the accuracy of generated text.
Contextual Understanding: By leveraging retrieved information, RAG models can better understand the context of the query and produce more coherent outputs.
Fact-Checking: Integrating fact-checking mechanisms into the RAG pipeline can help identify and correct inaccuracies.

By addressing these challenges and leveraging the strengths of RAG, it is possible to create text generation systems that produce highly factual and coherent outputs.

Chapter 8
Challenges and Limitations

While RAG offers significant advantages over traditional language models, it also presents several challenges and limitations.

Data Quality and Bias
Knowledge Base Quality: The quality of the knowledge base directly impacts the performance of the RAG system. Inaccurate, incomplete, or biased information can lead to incorrect or misleading outputs.

Data Bias: Bias present in the training data can be amplified in the generated text, leading to discriminatory or unfair outcomes.

Hallucination and Factuality
Factual Inaccuracy: RAG systems can sometimes generate incorrect or misleading information, especially when dealing with complex or ambiguous queries.

Hallucinations: The models may generate text that is plausible but factually incorrect.

Computational Cost and Efficiency
Resource Intensive: RAG systems require significant computational resources for both retrieval and generation processes.

Latency: Retrieving information from a knowledge base can introduce latency, affecting response times.
Privacy and Security

Data Privacy: Protecting sensitive information in the knowledge base is crucial.

Model Security: Preventing unauthorized access to the model and its parameters is essential.
Interpretability

Black Box Nature: Understanding how RAG systems arrive at their outputs can be challenging due to the complexity of the models involved.

Other Challenges

Contextual Understanding: Accurately capturing and utilizing context is essential for generating relevant and informative text.

Evaluation Metrics: Developing comprehensive evaluation metrics for RAG systems is complex due to the interplay of retrieval and generation components.

Addressing these challenges requires careful consideration of data quality, model architecture, and evaluation methodologies. By mitigating these limitations, RAG systems can achieve their full potential.

8.1 Data Quality and Bias

The quality of data used in a RAG system significantly impacts its performance and the reliability of its outputs. Issues such as bias and inaccuracies can have far-reaching consequences.

Data Quality Issues

Noise: Irrelevant or incorrect information within the data can lead to misleading results.

Inconsistencies: Contradictory or conflicting information can confuse the system and generate inaccurate responses. Outdated Information: Stale data can produce irrelevant or incorrect outputs, especially in rapidly changing domains.

Missing Information: Incomplete data can limit the system's ability to provide comprehensive answers.

Bias in Data

Representation Bias: Overrepresentation or underrepresentation of certain groups or perspectives in the data can lead to biased outputs.

Confirmation Bias: Data that reinforces existing beliefs can perpetuate biases.

Algorithmic Bias: Bias can be introduced through the algorithms used to process and analyze data.

Mitigating Data Quality and Bias Issues

Data Cleaning: Removing noise, inconsistencies, and duplicates from the data.

Data Enrichment: Adding missing information or context to improve data quality.

Data Validation: Verifying the accuracy and consistency of the data.
Bias Detection: Identifying and mitigating biases in the data and algorithms.

Diverse Data Sources: Using multiple and diverse data sources to reduce bias.

Continuous Monitoring: Regularly assessing data quality and updating as needed.

By addressing data quality and bias issues proactively, organizations can build more reliable and trustworthy RAG systems.

8.2   Hallucination and Factuality

Hallucination and factuality are critical challenges in the development and deployment of RAG systems. These issues can significantly impact the reliability and trustworthiness of the generated content.

Hallucination

Hallucination occurs when a language model generates text that is factually incorrect or misleading. This can happen due to various reasons, including:

Lack of Grounding: When the model doesn't have sufficient factual information to support its generation.
Data Bias: Bias in the training data can lead to the generation of biased or incorrect information.
Model Limitations: Inherent limitations of the language model itself can contribute to hallucinations.
Factuality
Factuality refers to the accuracy of the information presented in the generated text. It is essential for building trust and credibility.

Challenges:

Knowledge Base Quality: Inaccurate or incomplete information in the knowledge base can lead to factual errors.
Information Extraction: Extracting correct information from the knowledge base can be challenging, especially for complex queries.
Fact Checking: Verifying the accuracy of generated text can be time-consuming and resource-intensive.
Mitigating Hallucinations and Ensuring Factuality
Grounding in Knowledge: Leveraging a comprehensive and accurate knowledge base.
Fact-Checking: Incorporating fact-checking mechanisms to verify information.
Citation: Providing references for claims to enhance credibility.
Confidence Estimation: Estimating the model's confidence in the generated text to identify potential inaccuracies.
Human-in-the-Loop: Incorporating human feedback to correct errors and improve model performance.

By addressing these challenges and implementing appropriate strategies, we can significantly improve the factuality and reliability of RAG systems.

Sources and related content

RAG Hallucination: What is It and How to Avoid It

www.k2view.com

The Dawn After the Dark: An Empirical Study on Factuality Hallucination in Large Language Models - arXiv

arxiv.org

What Are AI Hallucinations? - IBM

www.ibm.com

Addressing bias in generative AI starts with training data explainability - RWS

www.rws.com

Hallucination in Large Language Models: What Is It and Why Is It Unavoidable? | by Sahin Ahmed, Data Scientist | Jun, 2024 | Medium

medium.com

8.3 Computational Cost and Efficiency

RAG systems, while powerful, are computationally intensive. Balancing performance and efficiency is crucial for their practical implementation.

Computational Cost Factors

Large Language Models (LLMs): These models require significant computational resources for training and inference.

Knowledge Base Size: Storing and processing large knowledge bases can be computationally expensive.

Retrieval Process: Searching through vast amounts of data to find relevant information can be resource-intensive.

Iterative Process: RAG often involves multiple iterations of retrieval and generation, increasing computational overhead.

Efficiency Challenges

Latency: Real-time applications require low latency, which can be challenging to achieve with complex RAG systems.

Scalability: Handling increasing query volumes and knowledge base growth while maintaining performance.

Hardware Constraints: Limited computational resources can restrict the complexity of the system.

Optimization Techniques

Model Compression: Reducing the size of language models without significant performance degradation.

Hardware Acceleration: Utilizing GPUs or specialized hardware for faster computations.

Efficient Retrieval: Employing optimized indexing and search algorithms.

Caching: Storing intermediate results to reduce redundant computations.

Distributed Computing: Distributing the workload across multiple machines.

Balancing Cost and Performance

Trade-offs: Making decisions about model size, knowledge base scope, and computational resources based on specific application requirements.

Cost-Benefit Analysis: Evaluating the impact of different optimization techniques on performance and cost.
Continuous Optimization: Monitoring system performance and making adjustments as needed.

By carefully considering these factors and implementing appropriate optimization strategies, it is possible to build efficient and cost-effective RAG systems.

Would you like to delve deeper into specific optimization techniques or discuss real-world examples of cost-effective RAG implementations?

Sources and related content
Understanding Retrieval-Augmented Generation: Part 1 - BentoML

www.bentoml.com

What Is a Large Language Model (LLM)? | SAP

www.sap.com

8.4.   Privacy and Security

RAG systems, while powerful, introduce unique privacy and security challenges due to their reliance on large amounts of data and complex interactions between components.

Privacy Concerns

Data Privacy: The knowledge base often contains sensitive information, requiring robust data protection measures.

User Privacy: User queries and generated responses may contain personal information, necessitating privacy-preserving techniques.

Model Privacy: Preventing unauthorized access to the model's parameters and architecture is crucial.

Security Risks

Data Breaches: Protecting the knowledge base from unauthorized access and data leaks.

Model Attacks: Safeguarding the model from adversarial attacks, such as poisoning or evasion.

Privacy Leakage: Preventing sensitive information from being inadvertently revealed in the generated text.

Unauthorized Access: Controlling access to the RAG system and its components.

Mitigations

Data Encryption: Encrypting sensitive data both at rest and in transit.

Access Controls: Implementing strict access controls to limit data exposure.

Data Minimization: Using only necessary data for the RAG system.

Privacy-Preserving Techniques: Employing techniques like differential privacy or homomorphic encryption.

Model Security: Protecting the model from reverse engineering and unauthorized access.

Regular Security Audits: Conducting thorough security assessments to identify vulnerabilities.

Challenges

Balancing Privacy and Utility: Ensuring that privacy measures do not significantly impact the system's performance.

Emerging Threats: Staying updated on the latest privacy and security threats.

Regulatory Compliance: Adhering to relevant data protection regulations (e.g., GDPR, CCPA).

By addressing these challenges and implementing robust security measures, organizations can build trust in RAG systems and protect sensitive information.

Would you like to delve deeper into a specific privacy or security challenge or explore mitigation strategies in more detail?

Sources and related content

Addressing Data Privacy for GenAI solutions with RAG Architecture - Slickbit

slickbit.ai

Considerations around Privacy in RAG-Based Architectures - Sarus Technologies

www.sarus.tech

Mitigating Security Risks in Retrieval Augmented Generation (RAG) LLM Applications

cloudsecurityalliance.org